AMERICAN INDIAN FESTIVALS

A TRUE BOOK

by
Jay Miller

Children's Press®
A Division of Grolier Publishing

New York London Hong Kong Sydney
Danbury, Connecticut

For help in reading and writing these books, Jay Miller thanks Keri, Megan, Kaitlin, and Noah.

Reading Consultant
Linda Cornwell
Learning Resource Consultant
Indiana Department of
Education

Library of Congress Cataloging-in-Publication Data

Miller, Jay, 1947-
    American Indian festivals / by Jay Miller.
        p.   cm. — (A true book)
    Includes bibliographical references and index.
    Summary: Briefly describes some of the customs and practices related to festivals celebrated in various North American Indian cultures.
    ISBN 0-516-20134-4 (lib. bdg.)   ISBN 0-516-26090-1 (pbk.)
    1. Indians of North America—Rites and ceremonies—Juvenile litera-ture. 2. Indian dance—Juvenile literature. [1. Indians of North America—Rites and ceremonies.]   I. Title. II. Series.
E98.R3M545 1996
394.2'6'08997—dc20   96-13475
                                                            CIP
                                                            AC

    5 6 7 8 9 10 R 05 04 03 02 01

Contents

Getting ready to
dance at a festival

Celebrating and Honoring

Like their ancestors, American Indians celebrate many festivals. Each event is a way of keeping in touch with the past and of bringing together everything in nature—plants, animals, Earth, and sky—in song and dance.

5

In the past, Indians often celebrated having the food they needed, whether they gathered it in nature or grew it from seed. They held festivals to honor food and holy places. Sometimes, they asked for important things, such as health or rain. Other times, they celebrated special events, such as births or becoming a woman or a man. These are still reasons why Indians celebrate today.

Dancing the Hoop Dance
at a gathering in Canada

Arctic Ocean

Northwest

Pacific Ocean

Plains
Mandan
Pawnee

Numa

Iroquois

Southwest
Pueblo
Hopi Zuni

Shawnee

Atlantic Ocean

Papago

Southeast

NORTH AMERICAN
TRIBES

Gulf of Mexico

Caribbean Sea

Thanking Plants

Many festivals thanked the plants and animals that fed the people.

Every year when a plant food grew ripe again, people celebrated a Return Food ceremony. Women often were in charge of these festivals, since they took care of plant foods.

Pinyon pine nuts—
an important food

Long ago, small bands of Numa lived in what is now Nevada and Utah. They gathered pinyon pine nuts and held festivals to thank the trees and nuts.

and danced. Sometimes they danced all night. This singing and dancing was to make the trees happy so next year there would be more pine nuts.

Farmers celebrated the growth of the crops. They lived together in big houses and towns. So when they held festivals, many people came together.

Farmers all over the East celebrated when the corn in their fields was ready to pick.

They called it the Green Corn Ceremony. They held it while the corn was still alive and growing so it would know that they gave it thanks. They danced around a holy fire in the center of town. Women wore many ribbons and danced during the day. Men stayed up all night dancing and singing.

The next morning, everyone ate fresh corn. Then they went home and began to pick their own corn crop.

Dancers perform a Corn Dance in the Southwest (above). Corn is still important to farmers like this Navajo man (right).

Thanking Animals

Men were often in charge of animal festivals, because usually, men were the hunters.

The people of the North-west depended on salmon. Many believed salmon lived as people in towns beyond the edge of the world a long time ago. When it came time for

Every year, salmon swim upstream to lay eggs.

to go up the rivers, they turned into fish. The first salmon to be caught was their chief, since he led them up the river.

After the first salmon was caught, it was carried to the home of the town chief in a new mat made from cedar bark. The chief welcomed the salmon at his door and gave gifts to the fish. A holy man cut up the salmon in a certain way, and it was cooked. Then it was shared with everyone, and they gave thanks.

People of the Northwest believed that when salmon were treated well, their souls went back to the towns at the edge of the world. The next year, the salmon were reborn.

After the salmon festival, people spent many weeks catching salmon and drying them as food for winter.

Salmon being dried for storage at a fish camp

The Potlatch

In the Northwest, a festival called a potlatch celebrated many events. Potlatch means to give, and **many things were given at a potlatch.** The hosts were anyone who belonged to a house, all the people who had the same ancestor.

Whenever a house wanted to honor something or someone, they began gathering food and gifts. When they were ready, they invited the leaders of the other houses.

At the potlatch, the hosts showed off the **songs, dances, stories, and magical feats** of the house. Children were given names. Deeds of ancestors were told. Art works were displayed. The leaders of the house made many fine speeches.

The important guests had to remember all that happened, so that they could confirm it when it was their turn to speak.

Everyone was fed during these ceremonies. When all the speeches were done, **the hosts gave gifts to the leaders among the guests**—baskets, bowls, clothing, tools, and art.

The Mandans and other Plains Indians hunted buffalo.

More than one hundred years ago, the Mandans lived by farming and by hunting buffalo in North Dakota. Every year they held a festival, the Okeepa, to renew their world.

During four days, they acted out the story of how

20

their creator saved them from the flood. Men dressed to look like night and day and like animals—swans, snakes, eagles, hawks, bears, beavers, and wolves. Many boys played the part of antelopes.

The most important dancers were eight big men who acted like Buffalo Bulls. They were painted all over and wore real buffalo hides. They were supposed to be the spirits of all the buffalo.

Inside a holy building, boys and men fasted and prayed. On the last day, Mandans prayed for all the world and gave thanks for food and help.

22

Rain Dances

In the Southwest, Pueblo farmers needed rain. They danced
and sang for spirits called
Kachinas. These were not
dances of a few people around
a fire, like the rain dances shown
on television. Men wore masks
of these spirits when they
danced. They wore special
clothes, paint, pretty feathers,

Zuni Pueblo rain dancers today (top); Kachina dolls teach children about these holy visitors (bottom left); Hopi Kachina rain dancers in 1903 (bottom right)

and animal skins. They danced all spring and summer to bring rain to their fields. These dances are still danced today.

In southern Arizona, a more complex way of praying for rain was held by the Tohono O'odam Papago. Every four years they held a festival called Vikita.

Every town helped out. Special composers made songs for the town members to sing as they marched around the inside of a holy place. The men

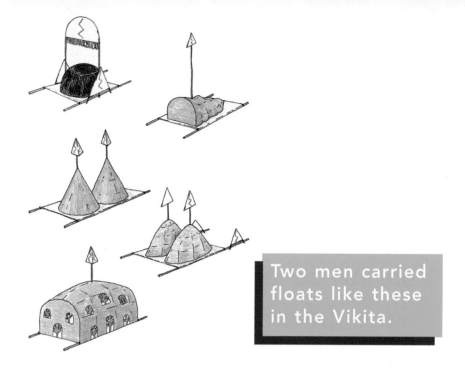

town also carried floats that were made from wood, plants, and cotton. The floats, which they carried in their hands like stretchers, represented mountains, clouds, food, and lightning. Each was meant to encourage rain.

Bundles and Holy Places

Every person and tribe had places that were holy. Year after year, members of a family would go to the same place to meet a spirit and get help.

When people returned home, they made bundles. Inside, they put things that their spirits said were holy. These might be bits of

animals, rocks, or plants. The
bundles held power that spirits
gave them. When people
wanted to use this power, they
asked the spirits. Spirits told
them how to use power wisely.

Towns and tribes had bun-
dles, too. These were passed

too. These were passed down from one leader to the next. Four sacred arrows were the bundle of the Cheyenne. The spirits who lived inside a place called Bear Butte (in South

Bear Butte is still used for religious ceremonies today—that is why there are cloth offerings tied to the tree.

Dakota) gave these arrows to the tribe. Two arrows were for men and women. The other two were for buffalo bulls and cows.

If one Cheyenne killed another Cheyenne, the arrows were hurt. They had to be cleaned and cured. Every Cheyenne knew to respect the arrows and to keep them safe.

Hills, lakes, and springs were holy to many tribes. The Pawnee believed that the spirits of many animals lived

Lakes could be holy places.

inside a few special hills in what is now Nebraska. People went to these hills to fast and pray. The spirits came to them there and taught them about medicines.

Staying Well

When a person got sick, herbs and bed rest were used as a cure. If the person was very sick, native doctors or shamans were asked to come. These doctors knew all kinds of medicines to try. They sang and drummed to call on spirits to help cure the patient.

Iroquois had many kinds of shamans. Some of the most powerful belonged to special schools of healing. They wore carved wooden masks and used rattles made of turtle shells. They cured with special songs and ashes.

When the patient was well, however, he or she had to join the school of that False Face. By being cured, the person had learned its teachings and so had to join.

An Iroquois False Face mask (left); turtle rattles used in False Face ceremonies (below)

Once a year, for a whole month, the Pawnee held a festival of all the shamans. It was called the Big Doctoring. A house was made ready. The shamans met there each night. They dressed and acted like the animals that gave them help. They used their power to cure people who were sick. After this ceremony, the Pawnee felt safe and protected.

Special Times in People's Lives

Every important event in the life of a native person was a cause for a celebration, sometimes just for the family, sometimes for everyone in the town.

Some of these events were birth, naming, marriage, and giving fine gifts. American Indians did not celebrate

birthdays until they learned about dates on a calendar. They kept track of time by watching seasons change and plants and animals grow.

Mostly, they had festivals when a child did something

for the first time. Most tribes made a big event of the first food that a son or daughter brought home. When a boy's voice changed, his family celebrated with friends and relatives. They did the same when a girl came of age.

At a wedding, the bride carried plant foods, and the groom brought meat. They made sure that everyone was invited to eat

A Navajo bride and groom eat together.

well. When a child was born, food was given to everyone who came to meet the baby. When the baby was named, a big party was held. Everyone in town had to learn the new name.

When someone died, all those who came to mourn were fed. Some families had a dinner every year for their dead relatives. These festivals were called memorials.

At Shawnee memorials, families cooked the favorite foods of the deceased. Family members were chosen to eat this food in honor of their ancestors. The Shawnee believed that while they ate the food, their dead relatives ate the steam that rose

Gifts are given away in a memorial (above). Food is an important part of a festival (right).

from the food.

The Shawnee thanked the dead for the good they did when they were alive. They also thanked the food.

Today, memorials are still held in many American Indian communities.

41

Today

Most wild foods are gone now
from North America,
and American Indians do not
live as their ancestors did.
However, many foods remain
an important part of American
Indian festivals today.

These festivals still bring
many people together to sing,

People dance and share food at today's festivals. Some festivals must be kept private.

NOTICE!
ALL CEREMONIES ARE CLOSED TO NON-INDIANS

dance, and pray. It is a meaningful time for people who still share and believe in giving thanks. It is a special time for those who still believe in the power of the spirits to help make the world a better place.

43

To Find Out More

Here are some additional resources to help you learn more about American Indian festivals:

 **Books**

Ancona, George. **Powwow.** Harcourt Brace Jovanovich, 1993.

Braine, Susan. **Drumbeat . . . Heartbeat: A Celebration of the Powwow.** Lerner Publications, 1995.

Liptak, Karen. **North American Indian Ceremonies.** Franklin Watts, 1992.

Pennington, Daniel. **Itse Sulu: Cherokee Harvest Festival.** Charlesbridge, 1994.

 **Organizations**

American Indian Heritage Foundation
6051 Arlington Blvd.
Falls Church, VA 22044
(202) 463-4267

National Native American Co-op
Native American Trade and Information Center
P.O. Box 1000
San Carlos, AZ 85550-0301

Powwows and festivals are held all over North America; your librarian can help you find out how to contact local organizations and tribes.

Online Sites

American Indian Celebration Powwow

http://www.wisdomkeeers.org/etil/etilpowwow.htm

Maintained by the East Tennessee Indian League, this site gives extensive information about pow-wows, powwow etiquette, dances (and dance styles), and songs.

The Green Corn Festival

http://www.whitestareagle.com/natlit/greatser.htm

Students who want to know more about this festival will find information here.

Pinyon Pine Nuts

http://www.desertusa.com/mag98/nov/papr/nov_lil.html

This nested page within the Desert USA site includes background on the importance of pinyon pine nuts in native cultures, how to harvest and prepare the nuts, and recipes.

Powwow: Dances

http://www.ktca.org/powwow/dances.html

Features the men's traditional dance, women's traditional dance, men's grass dance, women's jingle dress, men's fancy dance, and the women's fancy shawl dance

Important Words

ancestor a relative from long ago

bundle a sacred collection of items with special powers or meanings

celebrate show pleasure by coming together at a special event

ceremony actions done in a formal, planned way

festival an event to honor or praise someone or something

holy sacred, awesome, special

honor show respect

sacred set apart for religious use

shaman a native doctor in contact with spirits

spirit an invisible being with power over natural events

Index

Meet the Author

Jay Miller lives in Seattle, visiting nearby reservations, mountains, streams, and the Pacific Ocean. He enjoys eating salmon and pie, hiking in the mountains, and kayaking along the shore as much as he enjoys being a writer, professor, and lecturer. He has taught in colleges in the United States and Canada. He belongs to the Delaware Wolf clan and has attended most of the festivals described in this book. His family is delightful and very complex. He has also authored *American Indian Families, American Indian Foods,* and *American Indian Games* for the True Book series.